Couponing for Beginners:

Powerful Saving Strategies that will Save you Thousands a Year Using Coupons

Table of Contents

Introduction

I want to thank you and congratulate you for downloading the book "*Couponing for Beginners: Powerful Saving Strategies that will Save you Thousands a Year Using Coupons*".

This book contains proven steps and strategies on how to become a truly discerning couponer who knows how to save thousands of money using coupons without sacrificing personal time and money. Through this book, you will not only learn the basics of couponing and how you can become an expert couponer but you will also learn how to perform cost-benefit analysis that will enable you to see if the savings you get from couponing is greater that time, money and effort that you put into the endeavor.

Here's an inescapable fact: you will need to equip yourself with financial skills in order to achieve financial freedom and to provide the kind of life you wish for you and your family. Couponing is one of the skills that will prove beneficial to your quest for financial freedom. The powerful couponing strategies that you will learn in this book will enable you to save thousands of dollars per year.

If you do not develop your couponing skills, you will continue to use your hard earned money in buying grocery items when you could save them and use them in building the kind of life you want for yourself.

It's time for you to become an amazing couponer who knows how to save thousands of dollars per year just by using coupons.

Chapter 1: How Does Couponing Really Work?

Have you sometimes thought that you are allowing a store to lose some money when you get freebies from them? Or have you ever wondered if it is legal or decent to get freebies from stores using coupons? This chapter will discuss how couponing works so you can better understand it.

Manufacturing companies create various items such as biscuits, soda, toothpaste and toilet papers. These companies spend millions of dollars in marketing and advertising through TV commercials, billboards, and other advertising formats with the intention of making the consumers aware of their products. Coupon is really just another advertising format used by these manufacturing companies. They produce and give out coupons for their items not only to make the consumers become aware of their products but also to bring it straight into their customers' hands. They want their customers to use the coupons so they will be able to try out the products and tell other people about it. The manufacturing companies also spend money in making sure that the coupons are properly distributed in the inserts of Sunday newspapers, advertisement placements in magazines and even through online websites. The target is to have as many people gain access to the coupons so they can use it.

Once the consumers have the coupons, they can start using it during their grocery shopping. The cashier will simply san the barcode on the coupon during checkout and the price of the product will be automatically removed from your total payable amount. For the store to be reimbursed for the price of the freebie, they will have to send all used coupons to a clearinghouse who will then validate whether the coupon transaction is valid or not.

A coupon clearinghouse is basically an independent 3rd party who is not related to either the manufacturing companies or to the stores where the coupons were traded in. It is the coupon clearinghouse who determines the total amount the manufacturing companies have to pay to the stores. As you might have already realized now, it is actually the manufacturing companies who shoulder expenses for the coupon and not the stores. The manufacturing companies reimburse the stores for the total amount of redeemed coupons. But here is where an issue can occur: if a coupon is scanned for the incorrect items, the consumers will still get the items but the coupon clearinghouse will catch the error which can then lead to the manufacturing companies' decision of not reimbursing the stores for the erroneous coupon transactions. The coupon clearinghouse is also able to detect whether a particular coupon used is only a photocopy which can also lead to non-reimbursement. This basically implies that when consumers are fraudulent or deceitful in using their coupons, the stores will not be reimbursed for the transaction and that is when they will incur losses. That means that people use fake coupons are actually stealing from the stores. Because of the growing incidents of fake coupons, some stores have made the decision that they will no longer accept coupons that were directly printed from internet websites. The stores are concerned that some of those printouts are mere photocopies which could lead to non-reimbursement of their costs. All consumers are, therefore, asked not to photocopy coupon printouts. Generally, manufacturing companies allow the online coupons to be printed two times at the most.

But not all coupons are reimbursed by the manufacturing companies. The store owners themselves can opt to release their own coupons as a marketing tool to attract more customers. The manufacturing companies do not reimburse the stores for these coupon transactions. But it is actually possible to "stack" store coupons or store sales with the coupons of the manufacturing companies. We will talk about this in a later chapter.

Next time that you wish to use coupons and wonder if the stores will mind you doing so or not, remember that coupons are actually good news for the stores because they are reimbursed by the manufacturing companies (plus $0.08 per coupon transaction for handling). Even more good news is that the stores have more customers who will buy other non-coupon items from them. Coupons are also good for the manufacturing companies because they are able to bring their products to their consumers. With all the consumers that have tried their products for free, the manufacturing companies expect that a percentage of those consumers will purchase their products again even when they do not have coupons. The coupons are also great for you, the consumer, because you will be able to try new products either for free or at very good prices. Ultimately, coupons create a win-win-win scenario for the consumers, the stores and the manufacturing companies. You can use your coupons to get freebies in a totally legal and ethical manner without harming anyone in the process.

Chapter 2: Wholesale Clubs or Couponing: Which is Cheaper?

There are some people who question whether it is cheaper and easier to simply purchase your items from a wholesale store like Costco compared to gathering, clipping and filing coupons. Well, to answer this question, we can first determine which prices we should be hold out for with coupon deals. Here are some of items that a couponer should buy on sale or using their coupons: meat (including beef, pork, poultry and fish), supplies for cleaning, paper products, grocery supplies, drugstore items, hygiene products and baby products.

A comparison was made which showed that the prices of Costco are greater for hygiene products, baby care products and nearly all food products such as cereals and pasta compared to the prices when you use coupons. Some of the products compared are as follows:

- The Huggies diapers size 3 in Costco is $39.99 per bag of 228 or $0.18 per diaper which is higher compared to the $0.13 per diaper or ($5.50 per bag of 40) that you can get using coupons. The coupon price can even get lower when you use more coupons.

- The price of a 34 oz. Similac baby formula in Costco is $27.89 or $0.82 per ounce which is higher compared to the price of a 25 oz. Similac baby formula using coupons which is $9.99 or $0.40 per ounce. Both Similac and Enfamil give out fantastic coupon deals so it is advisable to join their mailing lists if you have little babies in the family.

- Bounty paper towels in Costco is $1.85 for each roll which is a lot higher compared to the $0.55 price per roll using coupons.

- Sugar can be bought at $0.56 per pound if bought in the biggest package at the lowest price in Costco. But you can get sugar at $0.30 per pound using coupons.

- The price of boneless and skinless chicken breasts at Costco is $2.79 per pound but they can be bought at $1.49 per pound during sale promotions.

- A set of 10 pieces of good Gilette razors will cost you $19.99 at Costco. You can get the same set for $0.50 using coupons. You can even get them free with special coupons.

But you can also score big deals when you shop at warehouse stores such as the following:

- You can buy cheese and other organic products at really cheap prices at warehouse stores.

- Some prescription medicines can be cheaper for as low as 40% at warehouse stores compared to the usual pharmacy prices.

- The prices of electronic gadgets and ink cartridge are rather low when bought in warehouse stores.

So there really isn't one right answer on whether it is cheaper to use coupons or to simply buy at warehouse stores. There are items you can buy more cheaply using coupons but there are also items that are priced low at warehouse stores. You just need to make some planning before you hit the stores so you can get the most out of your money.

Chapter 3: Become a Master Couponer

There is more to couponing than merely gathering, clipping and filing coupons. You need to have a good understanding of the different methods of couponing including BOGO stacking, catalinas and double coupons.

Buy One Get One (BOGO) Stacking

Some people can also get confused when it comes to buy one get one or BOGO sales. As the name implies, you need to buy one item so you can get one time for free. But do you know that you can match up a BOGO sale with a BOGO coupon to get both items for free?

Remember what we talked about in the first chapter? The stores will be reimbursed for the full price of the manufacturer coupon used by the consumers. For example, if the buy one get one manufacturer coupon is for an item worth $10, the costumer will only pay $10 to get two items. The manufacturing company will reimburse the store for the other $10 plus handling fee so the store does not really incur any expense. If the store launches its own buy one get one promotion or releases its own buy one get one coupon (store coupon), the consumer can use the manufacturer coupon together with the store coupon to get both items for free. The manufacturing company will only reimburse the store for $10 or the amount of the manufacturing coupon and the other $10 will become the store's own advertising expense.

True Buy One Get One Free Sale: In majority of stores, when there is a buy one get one free promotion, consumers are typically required to buy one item to get the other item for free. If a customer decides to use manufacturer BOGO-free coupon in addition to the store's BOGO-free promotion, he can end up with two products for free. The store will still receive a reimbursement for the value of the manufacturer BOGO-free coupon and they can still end up with a profit from the sales transaction even if the customer did not any money out of his own pocket.

If you want to use two of your BOGO-free coupons, you will be required to buy four products where you may be required to pay for two of the items to get two items for free.

But there are some stores who do not process buy one get one promotions this way. There are certain stores who require their customers to pay for one of the items so they will be able to take advantage of their BOGO-free coupon. Instead of letting their customers to get the two products for free, they will have to pay for one and get two products for free (one product from the BOGO-free coupon and the other product from the stores BOGO promotion).

Non-True Buy One Get One Free Sale: There are several stores who hold buy one get one free promotions where they do not require their customers to purchase two of the same items to avail of the sale price. A customer can choose to buy only one product and still get the 50% discount. If you want to use your BOGO-free coupon with this type of BOGO-free promotion, you will only pay $5 for a $10 product and still get another item for free. You can, in fact, get more savings from this type of BOGO-free promotion. Some of the stores that run this type of promotion include Publix (for stores located in Florida which hold the true BOGO-free promotions), Bi-Lo and Harris Teeter.

What are Catalinas?

A Catalina is a bit of paper that is printed out after you have completed your purchase transaction. There are basically four various kinds of Catalinas that may be printed for you: dollar-off coupon, manufacturer coupon, store coupon and preview of future Catalinas. A dollar-off coupon will say something like "$5.00 Off Your Next Purchase". You can use the dollar-off discount on any of your future purchases. There may be times when you will get a manufacturer coupon. For instance, if you have been buying Beech Nut Baby Food because it costs less than Gerber, you may find out that you always get Gerber coupons from the Catalina Machine because the system has identified you as a baby food consumer and would want you to try the Gerber products. But you would not really know what kind of Catalina will be printed out for you so it can be like a surprise every time you go shopping.

Target is one of the stores that print out Catalina store coupons. Rather than getting a specific discount (dollar-off) or brand (manufacturer) coupons, you will obtain a Target coupon which you can use on your next purchase. The good news is that you actually combine the Target coupon with a manufacturer coupon on the same item so you can get a bigger discount.

There are times when you will not get any of the above coupons. Rather, you may obtain a preview of new Catalinas that will be released in the near future. The preview will include details such as what discounts you can expect and when the promotion period starts and ends.

Here are some useful tips on how you can get your Catalina to release coupon printouts:

- Ensure that the Catalina Machine is turned on. Even before the cashier begins to scan the items you want to purchase, ensure that the green light of the Catalina machine is on. Otherwise, you will not get any Catalina printout at the end of the transaction. Even if the Catalina machine is turned on after the processing of your transaction has started, there is likelihood that you will not get a Catalina printout, as well. It is important that you check the Catalina machine prior to your checkout.

- Always double check the products that you are buying. So as to have a Catalina printout, you need to buy the correct size, quantity and brand required. For instance, if the Catalina promo requires a small bottle of Skippy Super Chunk peanut butter and you bought the bigger bottle, your purchase will not result to a Catalina printout. Therefore, you need to ensure that your purchased items are exactly what the promo requires.

- Contact Catalina. There may be times when you think that you have done everything correctly but you still do not get a Catalina printout. You have the option to contact a customer representative from Catalina at 1-888-8COUPON or through ncsc@catalinamarketing.com to seek assistance. Just make sure that the items you have bought together with the official receipt are within reach in case the customer representative will require you to provide certain information. If they are able to validate that you bought the right brand, size and quantity, they will be willing to send you the Catalina coupons via mail.

What are Double Coupons?

Before we discuss what double coupons really are, let us first discuss what they are not. Some people think that double coupon means that they can use two same coupons from a manufacturing company of one particular item. Well, that practice is not legal and it is not what double coupons represents. There are also people who think that you simply stack coupons (or using a store coupon and a manufacturer coupon for the same item) to do double couponing. Yes, stacking is allowed and lawful in a lot of stores but that is also not what double couponing is all about. Well, let me get our terminologies straight. You cannot really have or do a "double coupon". What you can actually perform in a lot of stores is to "double a coupon". This means that when you apply a particular coupon that you have cut out from the Sunday newspaper or you have printed from an online website, you can double the discount that you can get during days when the store has a "double coupon promotion". For example, if you have a $1.00 off coupon for a particular toothpaste brand and you use it during a double coupon promotion, the total discount that you can avail of from that one coupon will be $2.00 off. When a store holds a "double coupon promotion", they will only be able to refund the single price of coupon from the manufacturing company. The additional discounts given to the customer will be shouldered by the store itself as part for their marketing or advertising expenses.

Here is how you can get high-valued items for free by using double coupons: let us say that a 10-kilo pack of meat is $20 and it is on sale for $10 or 50% off and you have a $5 off coupon for the pack of meat. When the store has a double coupon promotion at the time of your purchase, your $5 off coupon will become $10 and you can get the discounted meat at no price at all! Whether you will pay taxes on your free items or not will depend on the store where you are buying from. But it is quite normal for you to see a total tax due on your receipt.

There are certain stores who do not advertise their double coupon promotions so you need to ensure that you regularly ask them about it. There are some stores who have double coupon promotions every week but only on specific days (typically, during their off-peak days). You can plan your trip to the grocery during these days so you can take advantage of the double coupon promotion. Kmart sets their double coupon promotion on a random basis and there are days when they will give discounts of up to $0.99 but there are also times when the discount per item can be as high as $2.00. Make sure that you regularly check their weekly circulars so you can catch their double coupon promotions.

It is ideal that you become familiar with the rules and regulations of your store with regard to coupons so you can be properly guided while you shop. There are some stores who only allows a certain number of coupons per visit which means that if their limit is 50 coupons for each visit or for each transaction, you will have to prioritize the coupons that you have so you can choose which are the top 50 coupons will give the most discounts. There are also certain stores which may restrict you to using only up to four coupons for buying four of the same products. Different stores have different policies as to the amount that they can double up. Selected stores only double the coupons that are $0.50 or below while others can double the coupons that have as much as $2.00 discount. And of course, there are those stores which will not allow you to use double up your coupons on items on sales or clearance items.

Remember that you greed is a deadly sin. Do not go all out and purchase 100 pieces of the same item and empty the whole shelf. If you already know that a particularly excellent deal is approaching, you can contact your store so they can order extra inventories for you.

Here are some useful tips on how you can make your shopping less nerve-racking not only for you but for the cashier, as well:

- Some cashiers are not aware that their store currently has a double coupon promotion. To avoid conflict and lengthy discussion, it is ideal if you can bring the flyer or the ad where you saw the double coupon promotion so you can simply present it to the cashier.

- Even before you get to the cashier register, make sure that your coupons are already out and prepared to be scanned for the checkout transaction. To make the checkout transaction to be completed faster, place the same products in the same place in your cart and in the same place when you put them on the checkout counter. Organize your coupons so that that they follow the same sequence as the items that are to be scanned. You do not really want to be frazzled while looking for the correct coupons while your items are being scanned because they are not in proper order.

- Hand over your coupons to the cashier one at a time so you can make sure that none are sticking together and the cashier does not miss scanning any of them. This will make sure that you will be able to get all the savings from your coupons.

Chapter 4: Save More with Coupons with Less Hassle

Gathering, clipping and filing coupons can really be tedious and time-consuming. Before you know it, you may be spending a lot of your time with couponing in order to get the same discounts as the Extreme Couponers get that you have no more time for your family and friends. Here are some creative and ingenious tips on how you can save time couponing but still make great savings:

- If you have friends who also use coupons, you can work with to save time in clipping coupons. Each of you can be assigned a specific coupon to clip so you can pile the same pages together and clip three to four copies at the same time. Every Sunday, for example, you and your friends can meet for a couple of minutes to distribute the coupons to be clipped (for example, you can clip all of the Smart Source inserts while another will clip all the Red Plum inserts and another will clip all the P&G inserts). And then, in the same afternoon of the following day, you can meet again for a couple of minutes so you each of you can re-distribute the clipped coupons.

- If a particular store is quite far from your home, you can work with a friend so you can alternate weeks to go to that store. For instance, this week, your friend will be the designated shopper in Target and you will just have to prepare a list of all the deals that you want to purchase and hand it over to your friend together with the properly compiled coupons. The following week, you can then be the designated shopper and it will be your friend who will prepare the list and coupon file for you. You can also opt to go to one store (ex. Target) for a friend while your friend goes to a different store (ex. Walgreens) for you. The important thing is to ensure that the list and the coupons are properly organized so it will be easy for both of you to purchase items for each other. It is also ideal if you can get separate receipts while checking out at the counter so it will be easy for you to reimburse each other. You will not have to spend time marking which items are for whom and then adding up the total and applying the sales tax. Having separate receipts will also ensure that each of you have a copy of the receipts so you can submit them for rebates in the future. Keep an organized file of your shopping receipts so they can be easily accessible when you receive a rebate form for items that you have purchased in the past.

- Collect the various ads for discounts or deals that you want to avail of and then do a price match against the prices at Target or Wal-Mart. Keep in mind that the following will not be able to be price matched when the exact prices are not included in the list: Rite Aid Single Check Rebate, Register Reward of Walgreen, Buy One Get One Free, among others.

- You can opt to avail of the services of a coupon clipping company. These coupon clipping companies are a wonderful resource where you can order your preferred coupons in large quantities. Rather than buying several newspapers just to get one or two coupons for hot deals which you want to get in huge quantities (such as coupons for buying baby diapers), you can simply place an order for those coupons with a coupon clipping company. Preparing to shop during Black Friday is another good occasion for ordering coupons. When you place an order from a coupon clipping company, you will not have to pay for the coupons itself but for the time spent by the company in clipping the coupons for you. Make sure that you do not pay the actual value of the coupon or more to the coupon clipping company because that will just offset all the savings that you can get from the coupons. Just keep in mind that it make take several days from the time you order the coupons to the actual time that they will be delivered to your doorstep.

- You can also join a coupon train which is an excellent way to trade the coupons that you cannot use for the coupons that you want to use. The leader who will start the coupon train will have to gather coupons that she does not plan to use anymore that are worth at least $100. She can then go to an online forum where she can post a message that she is creating a new coupon train and that she is looking for riders. Those who want to become riders or members of the coupon train will have to send a private message to the leader that will include their name and postal address (where the coupons will be mailed) and any list of coupons that they wish to get.

The coupon train leader will then create a sheet that summarizes all the information and will then send it together with her coupons to the 1st rider on the list in an envelope. The 1st rider will then take from the envelope the coupons that she wants to use and replace them with new coupons that she will not use but of equal or more value. The 1st rider will also have to take out expired coupons from the envelope to ensure that the coupons in the train are all still valid. The 1st rider will then mail the envelope to the 2nd rider on the list and the cycle will continue until the envelope reaches the leader and they can start over another coupon train.

Here are simple rules that the coupon train members should follow to ensure that every rider in the train get to benefit from it. Do not put in coupons that are about to expire. Do not pack the train envelope with duplicate coupons. Pay heed to the "wish lists" of the other train riders and make the effort to include the coupons that they prefer to have. Make sure that you get the train envelope back in the mail as soon as you can so everyone can benefit from the coupons on a timely basis.

Because of the Extreme Couponing shows on TV, many people has started to consider couponing themselves. But for a lot of people, couponing seems extreme and very complicated. But it does not really have to be that complicated but you will need to spend some time to learn how couponing really works. You also need to realize that you will have to make certain changes in your lifestyle to accommodate couponing and take advantage of the savings it can offer. Don't expect to pay only $5 or even less for a $1,000 grocery bill that you can see extreme couponers do on TV. What you can expect is that you will go through several trials and errors as you are learning the ropes in the field of couponing. Keep in mind that couponing is not one of the "get rich quick schemes" that you are looking for. Couponing can be considered as a lifestyle which cannot be built in an instant and without putting your full heart into it. The first step that you can do to make sure that you become successful in couponing is to print and study the coupon policies of your favorite stores so you will be guided accordingly. You cannot really expect to get big savings by merely showing up at the grocery store. Those extreme couponers that you see on TV are able to get their big savings because of their experiencing in couponing itself and their willingness to learn and become good at couponing.

Begin with just one store.

To avoid being overwhelmed, it is ideal if you will start to coupon at one store only. Different stores have different coupon policies and procedures and your risks of failure are very high if you attempt to start to get good coupon deals from five different stores. What you can do to increase your chances of success is to choose only one store and spend some time to study their coupon policies and rules. During your preparation time, you also opt to go shopping in that store to become more familiar with their procedures. You also need to keep reminding yourself that you do not really have to get your hand on all the great deals. It is alright if you miss a couple of deals or so. You do not really want to spend more gas money because you decide to go shopping just in order to take advantage of one good deal. Even expert couponers miss some good deals but in the end, they still saving big amounts of money. And believe me that the deals normally come around repeatedly so do not feel down when you miss a deal the first time. After you have mastered couponing in one store, you can proceed to learning how to coupon in a second store. Continue adding more stores into your expertise so you can take advantage of the savings that couponing offers.

Now, your question may be which particular store you should choose as your first to store to practice couponing with. Well, I highly recommended that you do not select Sam's or other wholesale clubs. It is ideal if you can choose one of the following depending on two things: your needs and proximity of the store to your house:

1. You can choose from to start couponing with a drugstore. The most common choices are Walgreens, CVS or Rite Aid. You can get health and beauty products for free almost every week. But you need to be aware that the coupon rules and policies of drugstores are the hardest to learn so you may need extra time in reading and understanding them.

2. You can also choose a high-end grocery store near you. Yes, these high-end stores may have higher everyday prices but they can also have the best coupon deals. They actually offer those great deals to entice customers to get inside their stores with the

hope that the customers will make impulse purchases once they are inside. So you need to control yourself and stick to only what you plan to buy and nothing more. Some of the stores you can choose from include Kroger, Safeway, Publix and Albertson's.

3. You can also start with a supercenter such as Target or Wal-Mart. These supercenters frequently offer great shopping deals and their coupon rules and policies are normally simple and easy to understand compared to other store types. But you can't expect their deals to be as great as those that are offered by high-end stores.

After you have chosen the first store where you want to practice couponing, you need to make the necessary preparations for your first coupon trip. You first need to determine if you will have to buy "filler" products in order to get the required total amount to avail of the discounts. You don't really want to be forced to buy the candy bars that are displayed near the checkout counter because you were not able to anticipate the requirement. If you plan to shop at Walgreen's, you need to remember that the number of the manufacturer coupons plus the number of register rewards that you will use should equal the number of items that you will actually purchase. Therefore, if you are planning to use 8 manufacturer coupons and 3 register rewards to purchase 9 items, you will need to purchase 2 filler items. Don't buy filler items that you don't really need. At the onset, determine what products that you need and can be bought as filler items.

Chapter 5: Keep Track of Your Coupon Savings

Just like with the other things that we invest our time or money in, we need to make a cost-benefit analysis to see if the benefits you get from couponing is higher when compared to the costs (time and effort) that you put into the exercise.

We need to break down our analysis into three steps: first, you need to determine how much savings you make from couponing. Second, you need to determine the time, money and effort you spend in couponing. And lastly, you need to compare your savings and spending to see if your savings are higher than what you are spending.

For the first step, you can download Excel worksheet templates in the Internet to keep track of your savings. You will have a lot of choices but to help you choose which template is the most appropriate for your needs, we will discuss the gist of the process. To track the amount of your savings from coupons, you need to make sure that you keep all your grocery receipts so you can log them in your template. You can use the table below as a guide if you want to create your own template in MS Excel. The first amount that you will log (A) is equal to the total amount you paid for your groceries which is net of the discounts. Then you will also log the total discount or savings (B). When you add the two (A + B), you will get the total value of the groceries that you have purchased (C). To get percentage of the amount you saved, divide the total value of your groceries by the total amount saved and then multiply the answer by 100 (B / C * 100).

	A	B	C = A + B	B / C *100
Date	Total Amount Paid	Total Amount Saved	Total Amount	Percentage Saved

After you have logged your savings, the next step is to compute how much you have been spending on couponing. It is ideal if you can log all the expenses you incur for couponing such as the number of Sunday newspapers you buy every week and their cost. You also need to consider if you have been using extra gas in order to coupon. Do you frequently drive to different stores to be able to get your coupon deals? If your answer is yes, you should estimate the extra gasoline that you use so you can add it to your spending. If you are printing coupons from online websites, you should also incorporate the costs you incur from ink and paper. Some couponers have converted their big stockrooms as a room for their stockpile that can have several thousands of dollars in value. Because of that, it is common to hear extreme couponers say that they get insurance specifically for their stockpiles. If ever you will get to that point, make sure that you add the insurance cost to your total spending. Lastly, you need to also estimate the cost you incur because of the time you spend on couponing. This last part is quite tricky to estimate but you can use your own basis for computation. One example you can use is use $7 (or another amount you deem reasonable) as an hourly rate which you can use in computing how much the total time you spend in couponing is. You may think that you are doing couponing on your free time and it does not really cost you anything. But put it this way: you can use that free time for other productive activities like spending time with your family and friends or some other activities that can actually result to financial earnings.

After you have diligently logged you savings and spending, you need to set a regular time when you can perform your cost-benefit analysis. You can choose to do it on a monthly or quarterly basis. All you really have to do is add up all the savings you earned for the month or for the quarter and do the same for your expenses. In order for you to compare apples to apples, make sure that your totals pertain to the same period. If you see that your savings are a lot higher compared to your expenses, you can applaud yourself for doing a good job. But if your expenses are higher compared to your savings, you have to see where you could cut on your expenses. You can implement the helpful tips we discussed above to reduce your expenses so you can enjoy more savings from couponing.

Conclusion

Thank you again for downloading this book!

I hope this book was able to help you to better understand how couponing works and how you can become expert at it.

The next step is to review the steps you learned in Chapter 4 on how you can start building your couponing expertise.

Finally, if you enjoyed this book, please take the time to share your thoughts and post a review on Amazon. It'd be greatly appreciated!

Thank you and good luck!